D0231880

Essex County Council
3013021374311 4

9
months

Quarto is the authority on a wide range of topics.
Quarto educates, entertains and enriches the lives of
our readers—enthusiasts and lovers of hands-on living.
www.quartoknows.com

First published in Great Britain and in the USA in 2017 by Frances Lincoln Children's Books,
The Old Brewery, 6 Blundell Street, London, N7 9BH, UK
QuartoKnows.com
Visit our blogs at QuartoKnows.com

**The publishers and authors would like to thank Dr Pippa Kyle,
Professor of Obstetrics and Gynaecology at The London Ultrasound Centre,
for her invaluable advice and support as a consultant for this book.**

Text copyright © Courtney Adamo and Esther van de Paal 2017
Illustrations copyright © Lizzy Stewart 2017

All rights reserved

No part of this publication may be reproduced, stored in a retrieval system,
or transmitted, in any form, or by any means, electrical, mechanical, photocopying,
recording or otherwise without the prior written permission of the publisher or a
licence permitting restricted copying. In the United Kingdom such licences are issued
by the Copyright Licensing Agency, Barnard's Inn, 86 Fetter Lane, London, EC4A 1EN.

A catalogue record for this book is available from the British Library.

ISBN 978-1-84780-817-2

Illustrated in mixed media

Published by Rachel Williams • Edited by Katie Cotton
Designed by Nicola Price • Production by Laura Grandi

Printed in China

3 5 7 9 8 6 4 2

9

months

by Courtney Adamo
and Esther van de Paal

illustrated by Lizzy Stewart

Frances Lincoln
Children's Books

How to use this book

This book shows how a baby grows month-by-month from a tiny egg until it's ready to be born. Each month has an illustration of what the baby looks like and how big it is, with some simple questions to prompt exploration of how the baby is developing. If you or your child would like more information, turn to the back for more details about this incredible process. We have referred to the baby as a 'he' throughout the book, but you can of course choose to change him to a 'she'!

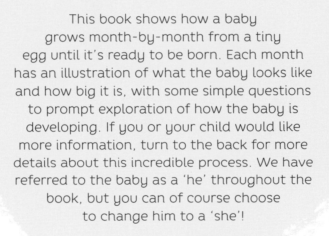

The beginning of a nine-month journey...

Can you believe that every one of us started as a tiny egg in our mummy's belly?
An egg so small you couldn't see it unless you used a very strong magnifying glass...

When that minuscule egg in Mummy's belly meets an even tinier seed – called a sperm –
from Daddy, they join together and a new life is made: the beginning of a new person!

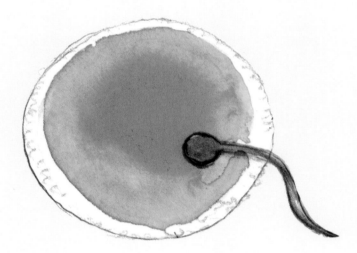

Even though the egg is no bigger than a speck of dust, it still contains all of the information that makes this new person different from anyone else. From the moment the sperm and the egg join together, it is determined whether the new baby is a boy or a girl, what colour eyes it will have, what colour skin it will have, and whether its hair will be blond and curly or dark and straight. Isn't that amazing?

This one tiny egg will grow into a baby made out of more than five trillion cells in just nine months' time.

In this book, we will follow this amazing process called pregnancy, and will show you the miracle of the creation of a new life.

Did you know?

Sometimes there happens to be two eggs, and both merge with a tiny seed – twins! Sometimes there are even three eggs, but that is very rare. One egg can also split into two eggs, growing into two identical babies. We call these identical twins!

A New Life

Once the tiny egg has joined with the seed, it quickly starts to grow. It travels through a tube in the mummy's belly until it reaches the womb, by which time it will have grown to the size of a grain of rice. The womb will be the baby's cosy home for the next nine months.

Did you know?

Not only did you start out as a tiny little egg, but lots of other animals did, too! Cats, dogs, horses and elephants, worms and snakes – they all started from one tiny little egg.

This month, the baby is the size of a grain of rice

What is a womb?

The womb is a soft pear-shaped pouch in the mummy's belly, lined with soft, fluffy tissue to keep the egg safe and warm as it grows.

How does the tiny egg grow?

The egg grows by dividing: first the one egg becomes two halves, then the two halves become four halves, four becomes eight, eight becomes sixteen… and on and on and on.

How is Mummy feeling?

Amazingly, all of this is taking place inside the mother's belly and is completely invisible from the outside. At this early stage, even though a lot is happening inside her body, the mother will most likely not feel any different at all!

The Early Stages

The baby is now the size of a blueberry and has developed a tiny heart, which is only the size of a poppy seed. He is slowly growing eyes, arms and hands and is moving with tiny, twitchy motions. But he doesn't look much like a baby yet – he looks more like a tadpole! He even has a tiny tail, but that will soon disappear. Inside the womb, the baby floats around in a sac of liquid, which keeps him safe and warm while he's growing.

month 2

Did you know?

The babies of pouched mammals like kangaroos and koalas are born after just 4-5 weeks. They crawl up into a pouch on their mother where they drink her milk. Then they grow for many more months, before they can leave the pouch and walk on their own.

The baby is the size of a blueberry

Why does the baby have a tail?

No one knows exactly why the baby has a tail in the second month. As time goes on, the tail disappears and the baby grows two legs, like you!

Can the baby eat and breathe yet?

The baby can't eat and breathe through his mouth yet. Instead, he gets the food and air he needs from his mummy. This is passed along a tube between the baby and mother, called the birth cord (or umbilical cord).

How is Mummy feeling?

Mummy's body is going through changes which might explain why she is maybe feeling tired, and a bit queasy. There might be some foods that smell funny to her, too.

A Big Head!

The baby is growing very fast! He is about the size of a lemon, and is starting to look like a real baby, but with a very big head – about one third of his overall length. Eyes and ears have appeared on the face, and the baby can swallow, yawn, and even hiccup! He can wave his arms and legs around, but he is still so little that the mother can't feel the movements.

3

The baby is the size of a lemon

Did you know?

Different animal babies grow inside their mummies' bellies for different amounts of time before they are born. An elephant will be inside for nearly two years, while a chipmunk will only be inside for one month!

Can the baby see yet?

Although eyes have appeared on the baby's face, he can't see yet. This is because his eyelids are fused shut. The baby won't be able to open his eyes for a few more months.

Why does the baby have a big head?

The baby's brain grows faster than the rest of his body, so the head grows faster, too! But as the baby continues to grow, his body catches up and he'll start to look more similar to how he will look when he is born.

How is Mummy feeling?

The doctor or midwife regularly checks the health of the mother and listens to the heartbeat of the baby. He or she has a special machine, called a scanner, which can be used to see inside the mummy's tummy and show a picture of the baby on a screen. The parents will see their baby on a screen for the first time, which is a very special moment! The parents might start to share the news about the pregnancy.

Moving Around

The baby is now the size of an avocado. He is very active and moves around a lot! He can now move all of his limbs and joints – even his toes and fingers – and sometimes he might even play with the birth cord. The baby is starting to look more and more like a person. He can turn his head, frown, smile and also suck his thumb!

The baby is the size of an avocado

Did you know?

Women are the only mammals with breasts that are there all the time. Other animals only develop breasts while they are breastfeeding, and they will disappear once they have finished nursing.

Why is the baby sucking his thumb?

The baby will practise his swallowing and does lots of sucking movements, so he is ready to latch on (get his mouth into the correct position) for the first feed after he is born.

Can the baby hear people outside the womb?

Yes! At the end of the month, the baby can hear his mother's heartbeat and voice, and even some sounds and voices from outside the belly.

How is Mummy feeling?

The mother's belly will start to become noticeably bigger now and her normal clothes might no longer fit. To get ready for childbirth, her body produces a hormone that makes the tissue between her bones loosen up. Sometimes this causes backache and pain in her joints.

Boy or Girl?

By now, the baby is the size of an aubergine and is kicking happily around in the womb. He is covered in a layer of hair, called lanugo, and also white, sticky stuff, known as vernix. The baby's sense of touch has developed and he loves to feel his face, or anything else he can grab. He can also now tell the difference between light and dark, even though his eyes are still closed. This month, a doctor can tell whether the baby is a boy or a girl!

5

Did you know?

Before elephant babies are born, they too are covered in a thick, downy hair. They shed most of this before they're born. However, young elephants might still have patches of hair on their head and back.

The baby is the size of an aubergine

Does the hair on the baby fall out?

Yes! The hair disappears in a couple of months. But at the moment, the hair and the white, sticky stuff helps to stop the skin from drying out while the baby is in the womb.

Do parents always know whether their baby is a boy or girl?

No! Some parents like the doctor to use the special scanner to see inside and find out, but others might like to wait until the birth and be surprised.

How is Mummy feeling?

The mother will start to feel the baby moving around in her belly!
First it feels a bit like butterflies, or like the bubbles you feel in
your mouth when you drink a fizzy drink. But soon they will become
noticeable little kicks, and might even be felt from outside the belly.
This doesn't hurt the mother — it's a wonderful feeling!

Time to Grow

The baby is about the size of a small pineapple but still has enough space around him to be able to move quite a lot. He now has eyebrows and eyelashes, and soon he will be able to open and close his eyes. He is looking more and more like the person he will be when he is born! All he has to do now is grow bigger and bigger.

The baby is the size of a pineapple

Did you know?

Kittens and puppies are born with their eyes closed and they don't usually open them for around 10 days after birth. Human babies will open their eyes immediately after they're born!

Can the baby breathe yet?

The baby is still inside the sac of liquid in the womb, so he can't breathe air yet. However, he is training his tiny lungs by breathing in the liquid, so he is ready to breathe air from the minute he's born.

What else is the baby doing?

The baby can cough and get hiccups inside the belly, and sometimes the mother can feel the hiccups. Hiccups help to prepare him for breathing as well!

How is Mummy feeling?

The baby is growing and Mummy will be carrying more weight. Her belly is now noticeable and round (her womb is now about the size of a football). Her breasts are also growing larger as the glands that produce the baby's milk start to grow.

Feel Baby Kick!

The baby can hear, touch, smell and see, and he can also taste different foods his mother has eaten. The baby's eyes will now have a certain colour, but it's very likely this colour will change after he is born. Roughly the size of a butternut squash, the baby is able to push and kick quite forcefully now! He is also growing a layer of fat to help him keep warm after the birth.

Did you know?

The blue whale is the largest animal on the planet and also produces the largest babies. A blue whale calf weighs 1,000 times more than a human baby, and is more than 7 metres long. It will gain 90 kilogrammes of weight every day of the first year of its life!

The baby is the size of a butternut squash

Is the baby getting squashed?

Even though his space is getting more and more cramped because he is growing so much, the baby can still turn around inside the womb.

Why do the baby's eyes change colour after the baby is born?

Many babies are born with blue eyes, which later become darker or change to brown. This is because of a dark tint in the eye, called melanin, which isn't present at birth but develops as the baby gets older.

How is Mummy feeling?

Often when Mummy sits still or lies down, the baby wakes up and becomes more active. The baby is big enough now that when he's active you might be able to see the mummy's belly move and jiggle! When Mummy moves around or goes for a walk, the baby is rocked to sleep.

Sleeping and Dreaming

Now that the baby is getting bigger and fuller (already the size of a cantaloupe melon!), he is too big to stretch out and is forced to curl up with his legs bent up near his chest. He will stay this way until the birth. The baby sleeps most of the time, and while he sleeps, he may even be having dreams! The baby is now putting on weight quite quickly, meaning his once-skinny arms and legs are becoming soft and plump.

Did you know?

Dolphin pregnancies last around a year. By the end of their pregnancy, mother dolphins are weighed down so much that they swim slower in the water than non-pregnant dolphins.

The baby is the size of a melon

Does the baby have hair yet?

By now, some babies have a lot of hair on their head, whereas others might have very little. The fine hair all over their bodies will mostly have gone away.

Why is the baby upside down?

Most babies turn themselves upside down because it is the best position for them to be born. However, some babies still have their head up and their feet down. This is called the breech position.

How is Mummy feeling?

It might be difficult for the mother to reach down and touch her toes as her belly is now so big! She will also find it difficult to carry heavy objects, and she might become out of breath easily as she moves. Mummy might visit an antenatal class where she gets together with other pregnant mummys to prepare for birth. They learn breathing techniques and different positions to use when they give birth to the baby.

Any Day Now...

By now, the baby is fully formed and ready to be born any day! What started as just one tiny egg nine months ago, has now grown into a baby. He will be around the size of a watermelon, roughly 51 centimetres long from head to toe. Even though the doctors may have predicted a due date for the baby's birth, nobody knows for sure when the baby will arrive.

Did you know?

Birds don't grow their babies inside them like humans. Instead, they lay eggs in carefully built nests and then keep these eggs warm until they hatch. Nests can be different depending on which bird has made them. A hummingbird's nest is the size of a bean but an eagle's is bigger than a bathtub!

The baby is the size of a watermelon

When will the baby be born?

Only five per cent of babies are born on their due date. Some babies are born up to two weeks afterwards! The period of time when a baby is expected to be born in a healthy pregnancy is between 37 to 42 weeks of pregnancy. This is when the mother has reached 'full term'.

Are all the baby's bones there now?

Most of the baby's bones are formed, but the bones in his skull haven't yet joined together. This means they can move and overlap a bit during birth.

Will the baby recognise his family when he's born?

By now, the baby will have learned his mummy's voice and the voices of the people very close to him. After the birth, he will turn his head when he hears a familiar voice!

How is Mummy feeling?

Like a mother bird prepares her nest before she lays her eggs,
the mother will also start to prepare for her baby's arrival, most
likely setting up a cosy bed for the baby with soft, clean blankets.
She will also have bought nappies and tiny clothes for the baby,
ensuring that everything is ready. And then she will wait...!

The Birth

When the baby is ready to be born, he is squeezed out of the womb and into a narrow passage called the birth canal, which has now become soft and stretchy enough to let the baby pass through. This squeezing happens in waves and can take many hours. Often Mummy will go to hospital to have her baby, but she might choose to give birth at home instead. Either way, a midwife – who is specially trained to help – will be there.

Eventually, the head of the baby is pushed out of the vagina, and after that the rest of his body follows. The baby is born! Now he will take his first breath of air and make his first cry! The midwife will check the baby, and weigh and measure him.

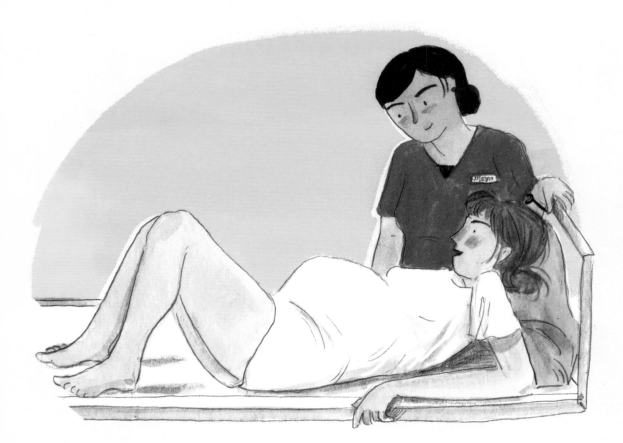

Are all babies born this way?

Sometimes, the doctor will decide that it's better to deliver the baby by a caesarean section, or C-section. When it's time for the baby to be born, the mummy will go to the hospital, where the doctor will make a cut in her belly and gently pull out the baby. The doctor will make sure the baby can breathe before they sew up the cut in mummy's belly again with tiny stitches.

What happens to the birth cord?

The birth cord, through which the baby received food and air while still in the womb, is still attached to the baby's belly. Because the baby is now ready to breathe all by himself, and drink milk through his mouth, the midwife or the doctor – or even the father or someone else special – will cut the cord. This doesn't hurt the baby or the mother at all!

Welcome to the World!

The birth of a baby is one of the most wonderful moments in life! Even though the mummy is very tired from giving birth, she is incredibly happy to see her baby for the very first time. She will hold her baby close to her chest, examining every detail from the tiny fingers and toes to the delicate ears and facial features.

For the first hour or two after birth, the baby is usually awake and quite alert. Often he will instinctively latch on to his mother's breast or a bottle and will start to practise and develop his feeding.

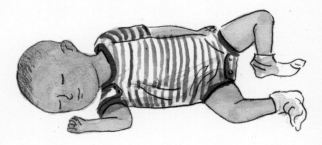

After the first hours, he will become sleepy again and will sleep a lot for the next few days. If the baby is born in the hospital, the mummy and the baby might have to stay for a little while until they are both recovered enough to go back home.

Because the baby's stomach is so tiny, he will need to drink small amounts quite frequently, which means he will want to drink milk often. Some babies show they are hungry by crying, while others will give more subtle cues such as sucking on their hands or smacking their lips.

Because the baby still needs a lot of care, he will stay very close to his mummy for a while. He will sleep most of the time, waking for regular feeds and nappy changes.

The place where the birth cord was attached to the baby's belly will soon heal and will become his belly button. It will forever be a reminder of the nine months he spent inside the womb, where he first arrived as a tiny egg consisting of all the information to become this one child – this little wonder we call life.

If you'd like to know more...

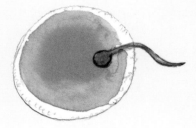

In the beginning...

Every month, a minuscule egg is pushed out of a little pouch in the mother's belly, called the ovary. That tiny egg travels from the ovary into a tube called the fallopian tube, where it might meet a seed, called a sperm, from the father. The egg is 'fertilised' by the sperm and this is the moment when a new human life begins!

Month 1

The fertilised egg, which is also called a zygote, divides itself over and over again on its way through the fallopian tubes. The zygote has become a tiny ball of cells and soon is called an embryo. It is tiny, but it has all the information to become a human being. After a journey of about one week, the embryo finally reaches the womb, which is also called the uterus. It is a pear-shaped protective pouch in the mummy's belly. The embryo attaches itself to the womb's soft lining in a process called implantation.

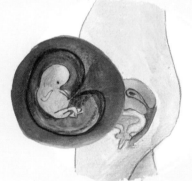

Month 2

The mother's uterus is a wonderful place for the developing embryo. The embryo floats around in a bag of liquid called the amniotic sac, which keeps the embryo warm and protects against shocks and bumps. The uterus also provides the developing baby with food and air through the birth cord, also called the umbilical cord. This cord is connected to the placenta. The placenta is an organ that not only transfers nutrients and oxygen across from the mother's to the baby's blood supply (the two blood supplies are separate), but also removes waste products from the baby's blood.

Month 3

The baby is now called a foetus. His face is beginning to look more human and the ears are almost in their normal position on the side of the head. Tiny bones are beginning to form in his arms and legs and he has even developed tiny fingers and toes. He is developing his own, unique fingerprints! By the end of this month, his most important organs and body systems are in place and the basic development of the baby is complete.

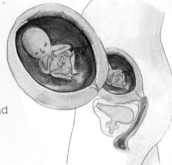

Month 4

The baby's body is growing bigger in comparison to his head, and his legs are growing longer than his arms, so his proportions are becoming more human. His hair, fingernails and eyebrows are also beginning to grow. His ears are positioned in the correct spot and his eyes have now moved from the side of the head to the front of the face. The baby's eyes are still fused shut, but his senses are quickly developing. His teeth have all formed inside his gums, ready to grow after birth. He is practising his swallowing and he is doing lots of sucking movements, getting ready to latch on for that first post-birth feed.

Month 5

The baby's body is now coated with a greasy, white substance called vernix caseosa, which protects his skin from becoming dried out in the amniotic fluid. His entire body is also covered by a layer of downy hair, which is called lanugo, and which will disappear later in the pregnancy. By now the baby's external sexual organs have developed and the doctor will be able to see if the baby is a boy or a girl by using an ultrasound machine.

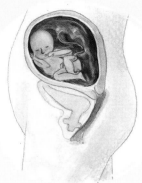

Month 6

The baby's eyelids are beginning to part and he will start to open his eyes for short periods of time. His nostrils, which until now were plugged, start to open as well, allowing him to start taking breaths of amniotic fluid. This trains his tiny lungs for breathing real air from the moment he's born. It's worth noting that for baby girls at this stage, an amazing thing is taking place: the uterus and ovaries are developing, including a lifetime supply of eggs. One day she will be able to make her own baby!

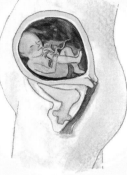

Month 7

The baby is now using all five senses. He can open and close his eyes and is able to see, touch and hear sounds outside the womb. He can even respond to different foods the mother has eaten. Because a layer of fat is now keeping the baby warm, the downy hair (lanugo) that was covering the baby is no longer needed, so is shed into the amniotic fluid. As the baby swallows the amniotic fluid, some of this hair also reaches the bowels. The bowels can now practise making the baby's first poo (which will come out after the baby is born).

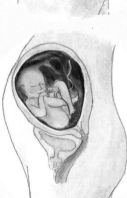

Month 8

Because it's getting very tight inside the womb, the baby is curled up in a fetal position. Most babies by now have positioned themselves upside down in the mother's belly, which is the ideal position for birth. Some babies, however, still have their heads up and their feet down, which we call a breech position. They can still turn around in the next few weeks, but it is getting more difficult. At this stage, the baby sleeps 90 to 95 per cent of the day! Some of these hours are spent in a deep, resting sleep while some are in the more active, dreaming state.

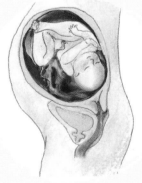

Month 9

When the baby is ready to be born, the mother will go through a process known as labour. Muscles in her uterus tighten and relax over and over again. This is called a contraction. The contractions get stronger and stronger and help push the baby out through the birth canal. The baby now takes his first breath of air and will start to cry. After the baby is born, the mother will have a few more contractions and will push out the placenta. This is the very last stage of birth!

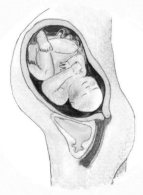

About the Authors

Esther and Courtney have been friends for 12 years, since the birth of their first babies in London, in 2005. As new mothers, they bonded over motherhood and the questions, concerns and joys that come with parenting. They have each gone on to have four and five children, respectively, sharing the nine-month journey of pregnancy together twice: their fourth babies were born within a few weeks of each other!

Together, they founded Babyccino (www.babyccinokids.com), an international family lifestyle website and shopping portal of children's boutiques. The Babyccino brand, now 10 years old, has become known for its genuine and stylish approach to motherhood. The website, which is updated daily with new editorial content and interesting parenting-related topics, offers inspiration and ideas for mothers throughout their parenting journey.

Esther now lives in Amsterdam with her husband and four children. Courtney and her family recently moved from London to Byron Bay, Australia.